The Wonderland of Poetry

By

Tripti Gupta

authorHOUSE™

1663 LIBERTY DRIVE, SUITE 200
BLOOMINGTON, INDIANA 47403
(800) 839-8640
WWW.AUTHORHOUSE.COM

First published by AuthorHouse 09/14/04

ISBN: 1-4184-9052-0 (sc)

Printed in the United States of America
Bloomington, Indiana

This book is printed on acid-free paper.

DEDICATED

TO MY

SUPPORTING AND LOVING PARENTS,

GRANDPARENTS AND GREAT-

GRANDPARENTS

AND

MY LITTLE BROTHER

FOR THEIR SUPPORT, LOVE AND

UNDERSTANDING

TO MAKE THIS FEAT

POSSIBLE

AND TO BRING OUT MY FIRST BOOK OF

POEMS

WHEN I AM ONLY 13 YEARS OLD

TABLE OF CONTENTS

FOREWORD

"I do but sing because I must "

                     - Tennyson

Poetry is natural sprouting as the flowers to a tree.
Poems by the baby poetess presented here are
simple, sensuous application of innocent ideas to life.
Delight is the only end of these lines. 'He who, in an
enlightened and literary society, aspires to be a great
poet' says Macaulay, must first become a little child,
he 'must take to pieces the whole web of his mind'.

Tripti Gupta's little book will enliven a few hidden
strings to music, I am sure.

Dr N.K.Gami

F.R.C.P(Edin)

1 BIO POEM

*T*ripti

Quiet, and shy

Friend of Naseeha, Dorothy, Simmarjot and Gurpal

Lover of her parents, her brother, and reading

Who feels and wants to get scholarships, become a

doctor and give her parents all the happiness she can give

Who fears animals, oral presentations and spiders

Who would like to see her parents happy, get good

grades until the end and peace in the world

Resident of the sunny San Fernando Valley in California

Gupta

2. MY FAMILY

Mother, Father

Myself and my little Brother,

We share our things and love each other.

I am the sister and my age is ten,

I have a little brother who likes writing diary

with his mighty pen.

My mother adores cooking and makes Yummy

Yummy food,

My father works hard and keeps our joyous moods.

We are a happy family and loves music alike

And when I play little piano, everyone sings alive.

My mother sings beautiful rhymes,

We pray to God for well being of all and happy times.

We like our neighbors and help them in their need,

And serve them well to be friend indeed.

We play in sunshine and dance in rain

Swim in our campus pool for a fun in-twain.

We have a computer at home, where I make

floral drawings

And play games like Wizard and Maze inns.

My brother loves Pokeman and Arthur puns,

We are a happy family and have lots of fun.

3 MY BROTHER

I have a brother
Who is beloved of my father and mother
He is five in age
He can draw beautifully on a page.

He, is very sweet
He, deserves a treat
He, is very intelligent and
He enjoys being a student.

His name is Anshal
He is smart
He is thin
I've never seen a better brother than him.

He enjoys playing with me
His favourite letter is C
I love him and
He loves me.

<u>4 WONDERFUL TEACHERS</u>

Every teachers is like a parents at school,
They cared and guard you, in whatever you do,
Our teachers educate us, in many new things,
They teach us, play with us and even sing.

They first teach us, our ABC's and then our 123's,
And other important words, like "sorry" and specially "please",
They teach us manners, we need to know for our succeed,
And tell us stories of many great heroes that have
done very good deeds,

They introduce us to students, so that we can make
new friends,
Because a friend is important in all our lives, for fun
and to defend,
They do things with us, so that we will always remember,
And give us beautiful presents at Christmas time in December.

We should always respect our teachers, because they
work hard for us,
And give them pleasant memories, so that they never
forget us,
When you are at school, you'll go through lots of
dead ends,
But when you grow up, you'll be really sad to loose them.

5 OUR GRANDPARENTS

Nanima and Nanaji,

Dadiji and Dadaji,

They are very special to us,

Without them there wouldn't be us.

They raised my father and my mother,

Who then raised me and my brother,

That is why they are called grandparents,

Which means they are the parents of our parents.

They taught our parents nice manners to be passed down,

Like to always smile and never frown,

To learn to except reality,

And take away our cruelty.

They give many things we like to enjoy,

Like candy, books, gifts and toys,

We respect them absolutely,

Because they love us and adore us like our parents, equally.

<u>6 RESPECT YOUR PARENTS</u>

Respect is like to pray,
You commit yourself to it every night and day,
You respect everyone - even your friends,
Teachers, other elders and most importantly - your parents.

Respect their dreams and wishes,
And travel together with them like schools of fishes,
Love and cherish them, but not in vain,
Worry not about yourself - your future and fame.

You must impress them with yourself,
And make them feel glad,
Because they have worked countless hours,
And given you all the fun you've had.

You should not let them feel at all bothered,
Because they are your mother and your father,
Because they wipe every tear when you cry,
And without them you wouldn't even be alive.

7. THE SCHOOL

School is like a second home to us,
Where we learn to read and write.
Arithmetic, Sports and even more,
And manners like not to fight.

We have special teachers,
Who teach us many things.
Things that may help us in future,
Or how to behave well with other human beings.

We learn to dance.
and sing a song,
The teachers correct us
If we ever do anything wrong.

School is a place of fun and excitement,
But whose dedication in a strong requirement.
It's part of our childhood we will always remember,
Just like many other memories that we'll remember
forever.

<u>8 MY LOVELY HOUSE</u>

My house is a wonderful place,
You can find happiness on everyone's face,
Our house looks very beautiful,
Warmly decorated and very colorful.

My wonderful mother strives to keep it nice
and clean,
She is a nice, beautiful, kind and not at all mean,
My lovely father works very hard for us,
He is always good at everything he does.

My brother is a cute, little boy,
"Pokemon" is his favorite toy,
To me, my family is the most important thing,
We all do things together like laugh, play and sing.

All of us work together,
If someone is having trouble, we help each other,
It doesn't matter if you laugh less or more,
It really matters if you live with the people you love.

<u>9 TWINKLING STAR</u>

Have you ever wanted to see something far away?
In the night, look up the sky and you will see the stars,
A star is an object, millions of miles away!
But, here from Earth, we can see it almost everyday.

Starts are extremely bright,
They are always full of light!
Shining brightly from above,
Full of light, it's what it is made of!!

You can keep gazing at the stars and dream away,
All through the night and all through the day,
When you look at a star, you will get a feeling of joy,
A joy which is just the same, when you get a new toy!

When the stars see that you look hopeless,
They fall down and give you a wish,
The stars are beautiful as you can see,
They seem to be saying, "Lets dream, just you and me"!

<u>10 THUNDER AND LIGHTNING</u>

Boom! Boom! Boom!
The lightning strikes,
It makes such a terrifying noise,
That I truly don't like.

It tears down the clouds,
With such a force,
And it brings down torrents of rain,
To the grounds that are dry and coarse.

Thunder and Lightning,
They occur mostly at night,
I'm sure this type of weather,
Must be very dangerous for flight.

Thunder and Lightning,
The world's most dangerous occurrences,
Sometimes when they happen,
The results are most damaging.

11 THE SUN

The sun, the heavenly ball,
The golden ball of fire,
It connects the Earth with the other planets,
Like a long connecting wire.

It gives light to all,
And energy as well,
To keep plants from falling,
And from night to dwell.

The sun awakes the world,
From the darkness of the night,
Each morning from the East,
At the West at night.

The sun is our key to life,
It gives us energy and light,
It grows the plants that feed us,
Wonder how without the sun, the world would be like.

<u>12 MY EARTH</u>

Our Earth is beautiful,
Our Earth is colorful,
Our Earth isn't empty,
It is full.

Full of Mammals,
Full of People,
Full of Trees,
That have lots of Honeybees.

The Earth has brown hills,
And lots of pretty windmills,
We have many mountains,
And many decorative fountains.

The Earth has seven continents,
Each with about a thousand cities,
And because of God,
Our Earth remains pretty.

13 SEASONS IN THE SUN

There is joy, there is fun, there are seasons in the sun

When we dance and play, for the happy merry day.

Everyone likes the four seasons

For many different reasons

Fall, Winter, Summer and Autumn

These are many seasons in the sun.

Winter brings in joy and bit of cold

As someone probably already told

This season is full of fun and holidays

With snow and laughter and very cold days.

When rain comes pouring down

And as you've already guessed

This is the season when we most enjoy & have fun

We play with boat, sand, castles and love sun.

And then comes mighty Summer

The season of heat and long days being warmer

The only thing is that it gets hot and hotter

We enjoy eating lots of juicy fruits and cold drinks

and water.

I share with you my enjoyment of the 4 main seasons

and others doesn't really matter

For now the seasons gets back to cold

And is soon followed by Winter behold.

14. THE SKY

The sky is blue
It's where the birds flew
The clouds stick together
In any kind of weather.

When the sun comes out
The sky is more brighter
But when a thunderstorm starts
The sky is more frighter.

The star comes out in the night
And in the sky, it looks very bright
The moon appears too in the night
And an aeroplane passing, completing it's flight.

The snow falls from the sky
In the day and in the night
It gets very chilly during this weather
You might not see a bird, or even a feather.

<u>15 THE OCEAN</u>

The birds are singing,
The fishes are swimming,
The leaves are swaying,
And the children are playing.

The mermaids are under the ocean,
The fishes and whales too,
Wouldn't it be much fun,
If we could live there too.

The water stays blue and clear,
If bend down, you can see the fish so near,
The Oceans are wonderful sight,
But try not to visit it at night.

Boats and ships sail across the sea,
To bring packages from my Grandma & Grandpa
all the way to me,
We enjoy breeze that the Ocean brings,
Especially in the mornings and the evenings.

16 THE BEACH

The beach is a magnificent place,
A place of rest,
Of peace and of grace.

The beach is full of brown, soft sand,
That leaves footprints behind, on your path,
The sand is strong enough though to build sand castles,
But to be made fast before it is washed away with a
"SPLASH".

The beach has a string sun,
Because without buildings to block it, it's quite open,
It's funny how the birds sweep so low to the ground,
And small insects inching away, praying not to be found.

At the beach you can collect shells of various kinds,
Once you go there, you can guarantee a peace of mind.
At the beach, there is so much to do,
It is surely to lift the tension off you.

<u>17 THE MOON</u>

The Moon is the most bright,
When you see it in the night,
It is visible, clear and nice,
Like a round block of ice.

It can change colors, from yellow to white,
It is really a very pretty sight,
Many other planets have more than one Moon,
So, they keep having full moons very soon.

Many planets can stay without a moon just fine,
While Earth has one, and Saturn has nine,
Astronauts get launched up in the Moon,
And everybody hopes that they arrive safely soon.

The Moon has mysteries abound,
It's really hot on the ground,
There you can hear no sound,
But large Rock easily found.

18. THE ROSES

Winter passes cold and slow,
And sweeps the world in a silent glow,
December passes and so does January,
I cal for spring to Hurry, Hurry, Hurry!

I wait for spring,
For a special thing,
For spring bring roses,
Bright, fresh, colorful roses.

Roses have a unique smell,
Smell it - then you can surely tell,
Roses are used as gifts as well,
The receivers always feel they are swell.

A rose might die,
If not properly kept,
All the cheerfulness it gives,
Will all be swept.

19. THE FLOWERS

Flowers grow night and day,
Facing the side of the sun's ray,
They are all over the place in May,
They sway in the winds, this way and that way.

Flowers grow, by starting from a seed,
Water, Air and Sunshine is what they need,
The seed grows into a stem,
And a flowers grow out of them.

There are many different type of flowers,
Yellow, Pink, White, Blue and Red,
Many flowers grow in a place is called pond,
And when winter comes they become cold.

Flowers makes people glad,
Anytime when they are feeling sad,
So flowers are beautiful by their colors & fresh smell,
This makes everyone's heart rejoice wonderfully well.

20 THE PLANTS

Have you seen a flowerbed in the plant,
With roses that are red,
And violets that are blue,
And other flowers that are fresh and new?

The plants will appear,
As they do, you can see them on ground so clear,
The flowers are so fresh in the plants,
On the days when you are sad, these flowers cheer you.

The plants will grow in various types,
And if they will keep growing, you will get fruit,
And vegetables fresh and ripe,
It looks very pretty when the flower grows in the plants.

The plant needs sunshine, air and water as their food,
If taken care, plants can be very good,
Plants can also keep fresh its neighbourhood,
With the sweet and nice smells from its flowerbed.

21. THE FRUITS

There are so many fruits, you can't name them all,
The sweet yummy mango is the king of them all,
Fruits are tasty and fruits are sweet,
They can serve well as a treat to eat.

Some are sour,
And some are sweet,
They come in many colors and sizes,
So there's always a variety from which to eat.

Fruits are healthy,
For your body and you,
They'll give you a good health,
And supply with vitamins too!

So eat many fruits,
At least four to five in a day,
That will surely keep,
The germs and diseases out of your way.

<u>22 THE HILLS</u>

The hills are tall,
Mighty known by all,
Above it, hangs the sun like a ball,
Come stand on it, you can hear the birds call.

The hills are shorter than the mountains,
Which is the biggest difference between the hills and
the mountains,
The hills and mountains are solid girt,
If you climb up there, don't fall but stay alert.

If cultivated crops bloom on the surface,
But watering them is what is the toughest,
You may see some signs of dead trees,
Because the forest didn't get enough water or enough
breeze.

The hills in the summer are brown in color,
But in winter, white snow makes it more prettier,
On the mountains, there is air fresh and clear,
And from up there, the clouds are much more near.

23 THE ZOO

Welcome to the zoo,
The home of the animals,
They live and breed here,
And grow their families.

The zoo keepers watch the animals,
To take good care of them,
So that they don't catch a disease,
Which might be harmful to man.

The zoo is a museum,
Of the different kinds of animal,
It gathers visitors everyday,
To learn and see them all.

Some are big,
And some are small,
Each unique in their own way,
But it is still fun to see them all.

<u>24 TEDDY BEAR</u>

Teddy

Cute and Cuddly

Friends of children, lover of kids,

Who wants love, protection and

a home.

Who feels isolation from other toys

and scary bunny rabbits,

who would like to turn alive and

experience life

Resident of toy stores,

of child's hearts

and of any home on the earth.

Teddy bear

25 THE CAT, PAT

Once upon a time, there was a red cat,
His favourite place was a black, old hat,
In this hat was a bright red mat,
This mat was put in by the owner of the cat.

A lots of people liked the cat,
Like a black friendly bat,
A kind brown rat,
And a bird that was fat.

The cat's name was Pat,
Many wondered how the cat sat in the mat,
Because it was only small enough for Pat and a bat,
It was also hard to find where Pat was hiding at.

Pat hid in the hat,
Close to the mat,
Watching a bird above which was fat,
And he just hid there and sat.

26 THE POEM OF LOVE AND CARING

Love your parents and their every need,
They provided you shelter, protection and planted
your seed,
The seed of your achievement and success in life,
Obey their every wish and let them not cry.

Love your brothers and your sisters,
You never know - they might have more wisdom,
Comfort them if they are very sad,
Play games, have fun and make them glad.

Love the nature around you,
Notice the changes in behavior and greet what's new.
Take care, water the plants and make the bloom,
For one day when you need it - they'll help you from
your gloom.

Love the earth and the people in it,
Make guests and visitors feel homely and relaxed,
Help everyone you can see, who are in need,
In need of food, comfort, water or money.

27 KEEP UP YOUR "HOPE"

Have you ever felt as if everything went wrong?

Your work went to waste- the one you worked on

hard and long.

When things turn out bad,

They make you solemn and sad,

But you should never give up,

Because, you must make yourself safe with the help

of HOPE.

Hope - what is it?

It is the rescuer of when you are deep down in a pit,

A pit of darkness, with no shining light,

A pit which makes you feel angry and unbright.

When you keep up hope, you rise and shine,

And when you do so, you feel just fine,

You keep up you hope and try things again,

And if they still don't work, try and try again.

When you keep your hopes high, you will always

succeed,

You'll obtain every wish, every dream, every thing

what you need,

So don't give up because the sun will shine again,

And you will recatch you familiar success train.

<u>28 CONFIDENCE</u>

Confidence in one's self,

Is one of the most important things of life,

because without confidence,

You won't try for anything to accomplish.

Anything is possible,

If mind is set on,

People have succeeded before,

So why can't you do it now?

If you have confidence in yourself,

You will be strong and daring,

Meeting and ready to fight all the odds,

That might have stopped you from winning.

Confidence is the start of success,

If you don't get the start, you'll fall in distress,

Distress - a place of losers that don't do anything,

Only because in themselves they didn't have

confidence.

You must have confidence in yourself,

You have to be big and bold,

If you know the correct way,

You can one day rule the world.

29 THE PRAYER

The greatest thing about life,

Is having one at all,

A chance to see the world,

The mountains, the beauty, the rivers and the waterfalls.

Different cultures have different ways of thanking,

They have various time as well,

Some do it daily and some do it weekly,

Some do it monthly, each in their own way.

All these are ways of worship,

To the many different forms of the one GOD.

All the Earth,

Must offer a prayer of thanks,

Its a way of thanking,

The prayer to GOD.

30 A VACATION

We are dinning,

And the sun is shinning,

High up on the hills,

Below the hill is an open space for the windmills.

We are going to Palm Spring,

And we hear the birds sing,

We see a picture of king,

A king who is eating a bird's wing.

We pass by a desert,

That is covered with dirts,

And has only sand,

And some brown, dead plants.

The desert always lacks in water,

Which is why the days are much hotter,

It is parchy and the hot there,

Because water is not available there.

You can also find some crazy shops in PALM

SPRING,

Look up in the sky, you might see, some birds flying.

We found some shops for toys,

And some that had clothes for girls and boys.

PALM SPRING is a great place for a visit,

If your legs get tired, there are benches to sit,

You should really plan to go there,

But don't forget to take your water there.

31 WONDERFUL MEMORIES

When the day is done
shadows falls
We miss you dear
most of all.

We miss your smile
Your cheerful ways
With you we have spend
our happiest days.

A beautiful memory,
will always behold
Of those who worth for us
can never be told.

Till memory fades
and life departs
You will live for ever
in our hearts

32 ITS A BEAUTIFUL MORNING

It's a beautiful morning,
It gives birth to the sun,
It's a beautiful morning,
The rise of the bright, the golden one.

It's a beautiful morning,
The wind stops to blow,
It's a beautiful morning,
The sun starts to glow.

It's a beautiful morning,
The start of a new day,
It's a beautiful morning,
Have a fresh new start today.

It's a beautiful morning,
It's time to wake up,
It's a beautiful morning,
Don't grump, just cheer up!

33 WORLD'S - A LOOKING GLASS

The world is a looking Glass
Stares back at you
When you Smile
Smiles back at you.

It gives everyone a reflection
of his own face
Very crisp and clear
without all thy grace.

If you frown at it
It is not a joyous land
When you extend helping hand
begets your life a joyful band.

So laugh with it
it will laugh with you on and on
Because if cry in despair
its not a jolly companion.

34 LAUGHTER THE BEST MEDICINE

Fate used me meanly

but I looked at her and laughed

Though none may know how bitter

fulleth was my cup, that was halved.

Along came the joy

and paused besides me

Happily sat besides me and said

"I came to see what were you laughing at thee"

Then comes the Laughter

bringing all heavenly smiles

Rising up and calling mighty heavens

and lurking the sadness behind.

<u>35 TRUE FRIENDS</u>

True friends,
Are like glue ends,
Once they stick together,
It's a bond of friendship forever.

Friends share emotions,
Between each other,
A happy one or a sad one,
Or something that troubles the other.

Make them happy,
And make them glad,
Help and be cheerful,
And never sad.

Friends give friendship,
A powerful gift,
It may once be the thing,
That lifts you from the ditch.

36. THE EVENING

The sun was shining brightly,
The wind appeared slightly,
The sun started to set,
And bees had enough honey that they could get.

The children started finishing up,
And had a glass of milk in a cup,
The mother's started cooking dinner,
Because now dinnertime would come sooner.

The father's packed up their belongings,
And the butterfly silently closed its wings,
Soon enough the doorbells rings,
And all the father's come in from working.

It has become night,
but the aeroplanes will continue it's flight,
Everybody will eat their first bite,
And after dinner they go to sleep and say "GOOD
NIGHT".

37 THE HOUR OF SLEEP

They say a cat nap is beneficial,
Whether you are a housemaid or an official,
It rests the body in a helpful way,
To have a small nap in the middle of the day.

It rests your brain,
From the daily train,
And lightens your head,
On your soft, comfortable bed.

Your muscles become smooth,
The stomach digests your food,
Your whole body takes a rest,
You wake up feeling you best.

A cat's nap,
You will see,
Will make you as happy,
As you can be.

38 I KNOW OF A BIRD "A BLUE JAY"

I know of a bird, a blue jay

I hear its wings flap gently in the wind

I hear its chirp through the trees

I hear its want for friends in nature

I know of a bird, a blue jay.

I know of a bird, a blue jay

I see its body glide through the air

I see its eyes search carefully for food

I see it rest on the branch of a sycamore tree

I know of a bird, a blue jay.

I know of a bird, a blue jay

I feel its absence when all is quiet

I feel its flight as I dream in the night

I feel the light of birds

I know of a bird, a blue jay.

39. BRIGHT RAINBOW COLORS OF THE WORLD

White and blue
Are the colors of my shoe,
Yellow and red
Are the colors of my bed.

Yellow and white
Are the colors that gives light,
Like a yellow sun bright
Or a white moon bright.

Brown is the color
For my literature book cover,
Oranges are happy and gay
And rainy clouds occasionally turn grey.

Some leaves of the trees turns red
These leaves are visible from my bed,
Many leaves are green, sometimes red
I watch them grow from my cozy little bed.

40 THE BOND OF PEN AND PAPER

A pen and paper,
Is the key of success,
The key that can open,
You from distress.

With a pen you can fill out,
Forms and requirements,
Essays, poems and the blanks,
Of your job application.

Without a pen, you wouldn't write,
Because a pencil is inappropriate, it wouldn't be right,
Pens come out in many varieties, each to suit your need,
So get out the pen and put it on the paper for its
regular feed.

Nothing would be the same without paper,
The world would be as bad as if filled with vapor,
A pen and paper are like, "Tom and Jerry",
The can't live together or without each other.

41 DOUBLE TROUBLE

Trouble troubles trouble
So never double trouble
When trouble begins
Always avoid trouble.

Get out of the problem
as fast as you can
As the best is yet to come
when the trouble begins.

Life is a battle
to be won and fought
When the victory is in the offing
all preparations are sought.

Our greatest glory
lies in life to behold,
Getting out of trouble
double up the positive bubble.

<u>42 LIFE IN THE CITY</u>

Life in the city,
Is different it can be,
From the traditional type of life,
In the good, old country.

In the city,
The streets are broad and wide,
You don't have to walk,
You can always get a ride.

In the city, people sleep much later,
And don't wake up as early as the call of the rooster,
Most business begin late in the morning,
And end late at night, tired and yawning.

Some buildings look like they pierce the sky,
Because most cities have many buildings,
They are so tall in height,
This is what life in the city is like.

43 THE ORCHARD

I have an orchard in the backyard,
A tasty one it is,
With guavas and mangoes and other fruits too,
And a small pond near it.

It has a few insects,
But for an advantage, I'm sure,
For the nourishment of the soil,
So that the plants do not spoil.

The fruit picking fresh, and eating it,
Is the most favorite thing of mine,
And I can do it easily because,
I have an orchard just outside.

I can pick fruits from it,
Anytime I like,
And it's no problem to care,
It even produces enough fruits to spare.

I LOVE MY ORCHARD IN MY BACKYARD!

<u>44 I AM A FLOWER</u>

I am a flower, queen of nature
I wonder why humans tend to smell me so much
I hear the buzz of a bee approaching
I see the sun shinning brightly down on me
I want to leave my roots and sail in the sky
I am a flower, queen of nature.

I pretend to keep still when people are around me
I feel the pain of when they pick me from my home
I touch my leaves in sadness as I die
I worry if I shall ever see my friends again
I cry when I'm unloved and wish to escape
I am a flower, queen of nature

I understand the emotions passed between nature
I sing the song of the birds
I dream of huge gardens full of beautiful flowers just
like me
I try to bloom every chance I can
I hope to rebirth as a flower
For I am a flower, queen of nature.

45. <u>HAPPY BIRTHDAY</u>

The balloons are hung,

And the day has begun,

It's your special day,

Which is your Birthday!

You get gifts,

You get prizes,

And many, many,

Big surprises!

You watch your mother make,

Your favorite type of Birthday cake,

And you watch the oven bake,

A cake that has duck in a lake!

The candles are lit,

And you enjoy every one minute,

You can hardly wait,

For this special date!

Because today is a,

SPECIAL DAY!

So have a very,

HAPPY BIRTHDAY!

46 FESTIVAL OF COLORS (HOLI)

Holi is a festival we all look forward to,

We eat lovely dishes and play with color too,

We pray to our God who is so good,

And eat our tasty, traditional food.

Holi is a colorful day,

Holi is a very well known holiday,

We play with colors both watery and dry,

And have get togethers and laugh until we cry.

In Holi we pour colors on each others,

And shoot water guns on our brothers and sisters,

Holi is a festival we really enjoy,

We cannot wait for next year to have some more joy.

47 INDIA MY HOME

I ndia - my country,

N ew type of life,

D eveloper of knowledge,

I n midsouth continent of Asia,

A country of pride.

When I went to India,

I saw a lot of things,

I enjoyed the fruits and vegetables,

Each special season brings.

On the road I saw cars

There were quite a few,

And many car- type bicycles,

Both old and new.

India has many special things,

Torrent like rains are what monsoon brings,

India's mangoes are hard to resist,

And before rain on mountain forms touchable mist.

India is my home country,

And I love it very much,

It has a lot to offer,

Both in single and in bunch.

48 HAPPY FATHER'S DAY

We all wish you a Happy Father's Day,
A day full of fun, mischief and play,
We thank our father for what he had done,
By doing what he enjoys and having fun.

We respect our father even extra today,
And let him win in whatever we play,
We give him presents of his favorite things,
And thank him for the love he always brings.

We give him watch, shirts and pants,
And anything he may like in his hands,
We take him out to eat at his favorite place,
And volunteer to even tie his shoelace.

We make sure he doesn't get bored or unhappy,
But always excited, lucky and happy,
We also make sure that he has a good day,
And that is all I wanted to convey on this special day.

49 HAPPY MOTHER'S DAY

Say hurrah, Mothers Day is here,
Have a wonderful day and give yourselves a cheer,
Things to do today are very plentiful,
So very happy and very delightful.

This day is made especially for you, Maa,
And for you to enjoy yourselves wherever you are,
For you to be respected by all of us,
Because you contributed your life, just for us.

It is made for you to enjoy your favorite things,
Like smelling beautiful flowers or riding on swings,
To spend precious time with your family and friends,
Or sit down jovially and play our favorite games.

It's the time we thank you,
For what you have given us,
And thank you for being a part of our lives,
And never forget us.

50 WEATHER IN CALIFORNIA

Nowadays the weather is hot,
The water can evaporate easily from a pot,
There is always a need of AC during the day,
This hot weather starts in the month of May.

During the night it gets as chilly as snow,
And in the sky we see a moon hanging low,
Sometimes it is very pleasant too,
Then you just can't decide what to do.

In California, it is very rare to see snow,
People go to parties and many amusing shows,
They don't have to worry about clearing snows away,
From the busy streets or the walkway.

Even though water goes up, it rarely comes back,
But here in California, water does not lack,
People swim in the pools almost 12 hours a day,
But to do this, they have to wait till the month of May.

51 THE DISASTER

September 11 ,2001

The firefighters rush to rescue,

In hope they will find a survivor or two,

Because the TWIN TOWER just got bombed,

Leaving New York City and it's people alarmed.

Many people had a chance to survive,

But many people lost their lives,

The day this tragedy took place,

Is on September 11th, on Tuesday.

Firefighters and police officers also lost their lives,

In helping as many people as they can, survive,

This event was a very bad disaster,

I hope that this never happen ever after.

They destroyed the city,

Leaving America in a pity,

I hope that this never occurs,

Not even the mountains or the rivers.

America will stand together, it will never fall,

It will be held together like a great wall,

No tragedy can bring America down,

And nobody can take off its crown.

ABOUT THE AUTHOR

A journey through the WONDERLAND OF
PEOTRY is a list of lucid and awe-inspiring set of
51 poems, which is written in a homely style, where
the work is striking rich in its originality and with
beauty of expressions by Tripti Gupta, who was born
on October 05, 1989 in the eastern outreaches of
Darbhanga, India, a world-famous place well known
for being ruled by famous erstwhile Darbhanga
Maharaj, known for his benevolence, humanity,
purity and prosperity, and a ruler of the Eastern Indian
Empire with his embellished grace for over 50 years.

Tripti started writing poems when was only 07 years
old. Her art became her persona and her passions
unfolded unto her delightful poise. She has already
obtained International recognitions and her works
are recognised, emulated and published into several

leading publications viz., Best Poems Of Poets of America - 2002, Indo American Heritage Foundation, Indonesian International Students Journal, American Emerging Young Artists, Americas National Publication in Natures Echoes, etc in USA, UK, India and South East Asia etc.

Her lucid works of dedications are admired and cherished by her teachers, friends and admirers alike, leaving indelible impressions in our contemporary life. This encouraged her today to publish at such a young age of 13 years, her first set of 51 poems as WONDERLAND OF POETRY , which is her tribute to Nature, Family values, Fun in Life, Our Hope, Life and Times, Lovely Habitat, and Events and Dreams etc that surround us. Her creativity has flashed Beacons of Lights and myriads of Kindlings. In WONDERLAND OF POETRY, her imaginations have reached astounding heights, instilling endurance, serenity, moving steadily towards highest pinnacle of liveliness and of mankind. This captures for us the thrill and pathos of beauty and optimism, with sanguinity in an inimitable manner.

Tripti lives in Los Angeles, California in USA, is a winner of US Presidents Education award, India Heritage award, Creativity awards, Outstanding Citizenship awards, Language Arts awards, Oustanding Studentship Awards, Winner of National Math-a-Thon, recognised as Highly Gifted and Talented Student(GATE) by LAUSD etc to name a few. She aims to become a famous Doctor - Scientist -Poetess.

Printed in the United States
24605LVS00001B/2